LEVEL 3

This is Spider-Man!

Based on the Marvel comic book series Spider-Man

Adapted from Spider-Man Beginnings, *written by* Jim McCann

Illustrated by Ron Lim *and* Chris Sotomayor

MARVEL

Los Angeles
New York

© 2017 MARVEL. All rights reserved.

Scholastic Children's Books
Euston House,
24 Eversholt Street,
London NW1 1DB, UK

A division of Scholastic Ltd
London ~ New York ~ Toronto ~ Sydney ~ Auckland
Mexico City ~ New Delhi ~ Hong Kong

This book was first published in Australia in 2016 by Scholastic Australia
Published in the UK by Scholastic Ltd, 2017

ISBN 978 1407 17436 5

Printed in Malaysia

2 4 6 8 10 9 7 5 3 1

Papers used by Scholastic Children's Books are made from wood grown in sustainable forests.

www.scholastic.co.uk

Chapter 1

Peter Parker may look like an ordinary school kid, but he has an amazing secret…

Peter Parker has special powers.
He is Spider-Man!
He can do all sorts of amazing things.

He can climb tall buildings and swing
through the air using webs.
Spider-Man helps people in need.

Peter Parker became Spider-Man because of an accident. He was in the science lab when a spider bit him. It was not an ordinary spider and the bite gave Peter special powers.

Peter found out that he could lift heavy objects! He could climb buildings just like a spider. He now had super senses! And that's not all – he could now shoot webs like a spider, too!

Peter is always ready for action. He hides
who he is by wearing a special costume.
When he wears it he is Spider-Man!
No one else knows about Peter's secret.

Peter has to face new challenges every day. There are many villains who want to make trouble and it is his job as Spider-Man to stop them.

When Spider-Man's foe, the Green Goblin, glides into the city, Spider-Man is ready to defeat him.

Spider-Man has to be ready to fight his enemies, wherever he might be.
One day Sandman looms out of the sand.

Spider-Man stops Sandman by
shooting webs from his web-shooters.
Spider-Man saves the day!

Spider-Man's special senses mean that he can sense danger. When he senses danger, he swings into action to make sure that no one is hurt.

Spider-Man has amazing powers. He can leap huge distances and move so quickly that he stuns his enemies.

Even Spider-Man's toughest foes can't
match him. He uses all his powers
when he is in battle. He won't stop until
he has defeated all the bad guys.

No matter how fast his enemies are,
Spider-Man is quicker!
He uses his spidey-skills to climb high
up on buildings. He can dodge even the
most fearsome attack.

Spider-Man is quick-thinking.
He can defeat his foes by using
his wits. He is a very clever hero.

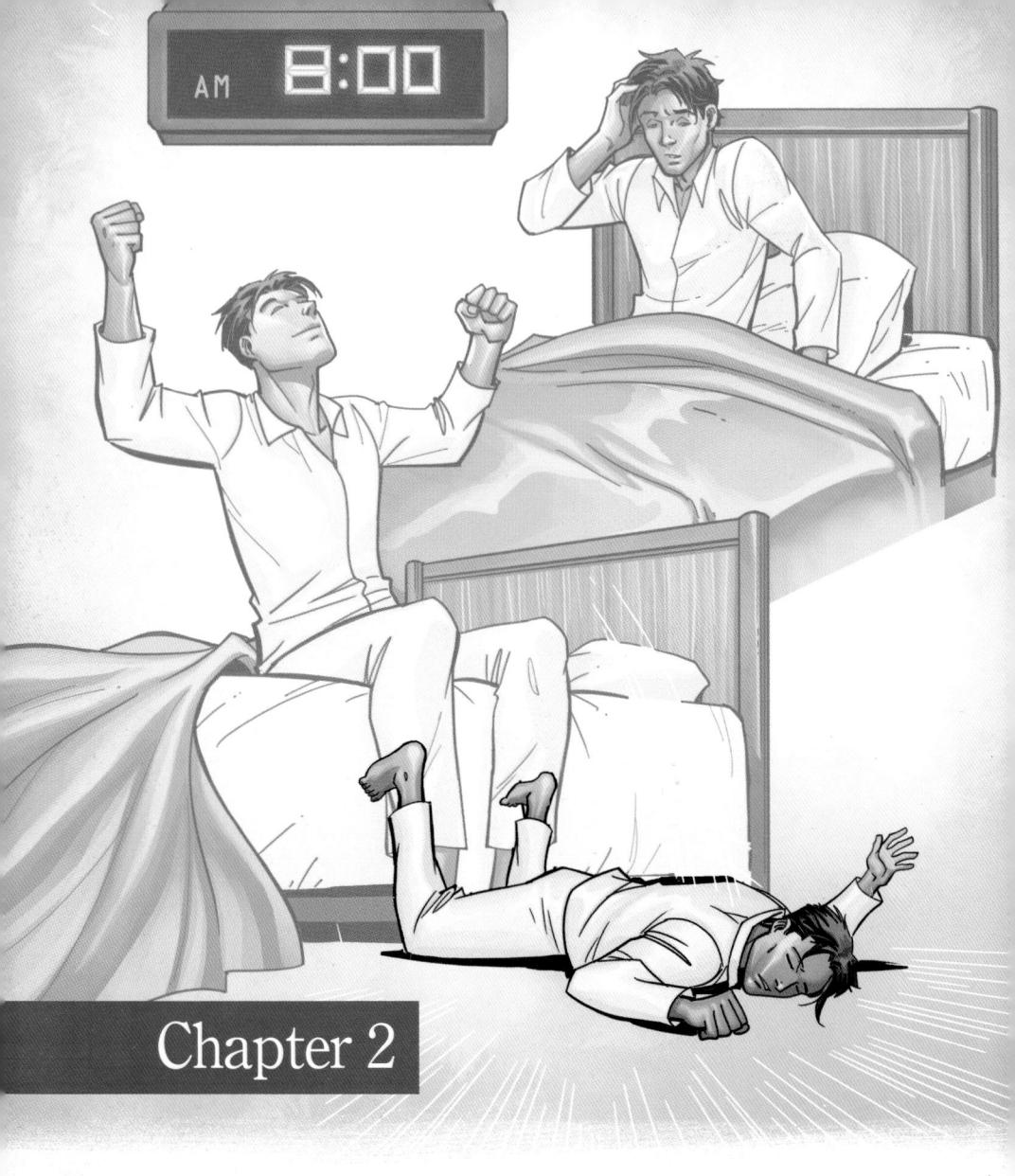

Chapter 2

Peter Parker is tired. He has been busy as Spider-Man. Saving the city is a very tiring job! But he has to go to school as well.

Mary Jane is worried about her friend because he looks so tired. Is he unwell? Peter would like to tell MJ his secret, but he can't.

Peter's classmate Flash thinks
Spider-Man is cool.
"I'm strong like Spider-Man," Flash
says as he puts on a mask. "I bet you
wish you were strong like Spider-Man!"
he teases Peter.

Peter's spidey-senses start tingling.
He can sense danger close by! He checks
no one can see him and shoots a web.
He snatches the mask Flash put in his
back pocket. Peter puts the mask on and
swings into action.

Doctor Octopus is waiting for Spider-Man. He uses his robot arms to hurl Peter into the air. Peter lands with a thud.

Doc Ock grabs and nips with his robot arms. He wants to catch this pesky hero. But Peter is quick and jumps away from Doc Ock.

But Doc Ock doesn't give up. Two of his arms grab hold of Peter. Another robot arm whips out. Peter struggles but he cannot move. A claw grabs his mask and lifts it up.

Doc Ock cannot believe it. The hero
is a kid! He is furious. He drops Peter
and starts to destroy the buildings.
Peter's classmates are in danger.

Peter is hiding. He has found his school
bag. Luckily, no one saw Peter's face
when his mask was ripped off.

Peter decides he must defeat Doc Ock!
He puts on his Spider-Man costume.
He makes a plan.

Then he hears Mary Jane shouting.
She is in trouble! Doc Ock has grabbed MJ
with his robot arms.

Spider-Man shoots webs from his
web-shooters and swings into the air.
He nimbly swerves past Doc Ock and
grabs MJ. Spider-Man and MJ soar into
the air and away from Doc Ock.

Spider-Man makes sure that MJ is safe.
"I must go back," he says.
"I have some unfinished business with
Doc Ock."

Spider-Man defeats Doc Ock with his
skilful moves.
"Not so bad for a kid!" Spider-Man laughs.
Doc Ock won't mess with Spider-Man again!

Peter Parker is no ordinary kid.
He may be resting now but he is always
alert, ready for danger. Peter is always
ready to keep the city safe.

Spider-Man can always sense when to swing into action and save the day!